AND IF THE DEAD DO DREAM

Poems by

Anita Sullivan

First U.S. edition 2016

Editor and Publisher:	Laura LeHew
	Uttered Chaos
	www.utteredchaos.org

Proofreader: Nancy Carol Moody

Cover: "untitled" © Tim Sullivan

Tim Sullivan is based in Alameda, California. He loves photography and travel. Due to these loves of his, he has turned himself into a professional photographer and an airline pilot. Tim enjoys exploring the world, and telling stories with his camera. www.timsullivanphoto.com.

Back cover photo: "Anita Sullivan" © Tim Sullivan

ISBN: 978-0-9889366-6-9

My mother was born beside a spring in the high desert, just north of where West Texas and Mexico meet along the Rio Grande. Born three months premature, she was kept alive in an incubator heated with household lightbulbs. An eyedropper was used for feeding. The water from the spring bathed and filled her body, tightening each of her cells. It filled the hollow of her bones. Years later, as the water passed from mother to child like fine hair or blue eyes, I grew up thinking that water and the desert were the same.

— Craig Childs, *The Secret Knowledge of Water*

The old remember being flowers,
but the young ridicule them and remember fire.

— James Richardson, "The Encyclopedia of the Stones"

CONTENTS

LEAF DANCING

Here is what I see. An asphalt road winding uphill ahead of me, dappled by shadows from late summer trees. As I lean the car into a long right-hand curve, a large yellow leaf, probably a Bigleaf Maple, skitters out from the left side of the road directly into my path like a pedestrian crossing without looking both ways for traffic.

Reaching the line in the middle of the road, it stops. It starts to spin— vertically, on its sturdy stem—so slowly at first, I don't recognize what is happening. But there is no mistaking that this leaf is fully upright, and that it could not maintain this position at all if it were not twirling, even in the graceful, distracted way of a gamin princess.

Quickly I check the trees on either side, the tall grasses beside the road as well. They are motionless; there is no breeze. The leaf is dancing for some other reason. It wobbles a little, like a lopsided planet—begins to tip – but then with a rush of something like desperate ecstasy, it rights itself for that last three full seconds of fandango panache directly in front of the oncoming metal bumper that will soon destroy it.

I blink. I slow to a crawl while the leaf completes its last pirouette, falls over and resumes a horizontal position on the pavement. Surely I have not just witnessed a blatant flouting of certain of the smaller laws of biology and physics! There may be no air moving in the vicinity, but I obviously failed to discern the maverick eddy prowling along the ground, small enough to lift a single leaf and make it into a temporary puppet clown. Right?

But no, I've seen this happen before, and this time the boldness and clarity of the leaf's actions finally convinces me. That silly, fragile, skittish bit of flotsam out there has carried out an act of frivolity in pure form.

I don't know if leaves need to break away and dance from time to time, but they do it nonetheless. And could these sometime surreptitious botanical outbursts be simply another example of Nature's normal habit of redundancy, experimentation, excess? Or are the leaves actually getting away with something unauthorized? Either way is fine with me.

GREEN IS WATER SOMEWHERE ELSE

One day water
stepped out for a moment
>   *after the hour*
>   *but before the minute*
>   *after blood*
>   *but before wine.*

Water went
somewhere else,
found

permission to be away without notice
there
without incurring
the additional stigma of absence
here.

A price was paid—a price is always paid—
On that day the jungle, the meadow, the forest
                    arrived, became
by courtesy,
water without need
water held
in escrow.

FOUR POSTS HOLD UP THE KNOWN WORLD

My old car bounces along the pocked asphalt
on the way to the store.

A harpsichord concerto comes out
of the radio.

Shadows flick like shuffled cards
from passing winter trees.

I see that the car in front of me
is being driven by my dead brother.

STARTING WITH GEOMETRY

The white convex strips along the squirrel's bent knees
as he sits
in eating position
                    perfectly balancing

white concave bands inside his elbows

Trim these curves
away from the small animal
let them float—perfect
                    geometric forms in air!

                                        Yet
this would not come clear
were they not fur

4

A TAXONOMY OF GRIEVING

Often I am stopped by the hawk's heart
then able to continue
        among the ivy.

Mortal peril steeps the air, yet air
being fickle, frequently slackens
                       (Bear to Lady)

Question: How can a plant and an animal
share the same parts?

Answer: On a roof

How far I have come after you stopped!
        Sliding past you on my allotted track
        I ride the soft yellow
                toe of frog
(I pause often, looking back).

You carry my seed.
I carry your eye.

MULBERRY

Shifting weight
from one foot to the other

to walk or run

involves tiny grains of intention
drifting down at measured speed

through the mind's hourglass.

The leap
occurs only as afterthought.

Such easy grace, no need to stumble.

All things [meaning not *things*]
configure themselves
      by their angles
           their gradual trajectories
                their subsequent projections.

At the bottom of the garden
      the bush
           the monkey
               the weasel.

Is that not how I have always loved you?

NOTES FOR A CONVERSATION I WOULD LIKE TO HAVE ONE DAY WITH MY SON SINCE I NEVER HAD IT WITH MY MOTHER

Outside the window, waves of chickadee voices
break lightly against the glass

The beagle next door barks once or twice
like breakfast toast popping up from the grass

"I want to die healthy," your grandmother always said
and sure, I knew what she meant, but

All my life I've thrived on these—
spontaneous visitations

Never having got the knack
of evoking joy on command

I save certain lines:
       a fading of ponies
       nightbollsnorted
       The watched toast never boils

That pile of crushed blossoms we must fall into
last thing, the very last no matter what

PRAYER OF A REFUGEE

And in the walls and streets of cities we lie buried
like bees in sand,
not ready to die yet, turning slowly
inside our discs of shifting patterns
through which our feet of thread
stab and stab.

Does anything ever stop?

If so, tell and I will go
to feel the stillness
suck out the teeth of me—.

A bowl of millet every morning under a baobab tree
between me and my death, and the steam of it
quakeless—oh praise! To make a stack of these,
soft, with no spaces between, and dwell
mute in the rooted shade.

PROBABLY THE APPLES

for Patrick

Now I see my apple-picking tool
leaning against the fence in November
as "a clawed hand."

And furthermore, with too little flesh, alas!

This might be the biology
of skin abraded
(the red paint almost gone)

the metallurgy of skin almost frozen,
the geology of articulate ribs—
sine waves at the waterfall's lip.

Truly, there are few configurations.

The eyes, for example,
arched doorways
                    with clear glass doors,
allow instant passage through the head
for blackberries blooming along a path

so that what is in front
is also, at the same moment,
behind.

It must be like this for him too,
after the infinite atom rises into
the finite molecule.

Everywhere he walks and sleeps
on city streets, probably the apples,
the blackberries

stay fixed after entering
the small room behind his eyes—.

9

Shallow curves surround him:
sink bowls, wheel-wells, smiles,
guitars, street lights, plastic chairs—

all might well be claws.

Countering this,
he keeps the glass in the back of his head
clouded.

THE LAND RENEWS ITS ROLE AS HORSE

Columbia River Gorge, Eastern end

An hour comes
when the streams
and the grasses beside the streams
and the trees beside the
                              grasses
          turn the same color.

They say this happens
whenever the sun
caught in the branches of Time's red tree
                    is torn
                                        to smithereens.

Back along the river, giant windmills
have sunk down
          into the clefts of grey-brown
                              hills
until only their blade-tips show
          like spinning crowns
                              of white thorns.

On this October afternoon
we wander the fields and
a pong hangs in the air.

Seeking its source, we see
          among the tumbled boulders
are sheep remembering
                    their eyes
were bequeathed to them by the ancient horses
as they were going extinct.

PERAMBULATION 1

If I were to say,
"Here is my cow, Nasturtium"

If there were such a cow
standing in a field tolling like a yellow bell

How could I claim her that way
without risking much more?

She might have the soul of a dragon

NETTED

Strolls
down the switchback trail
an obvious
sorcerer
with dark hat, hollow
stick who
sees me
up here
seeing him—
flares,

shrinks,
to slip into
his stick's
diverticular
throat

flies over me
into the forest
then leaf-wary
returns
by thickening

into a wren
riding the pinioned
exoskeleton
of a fern.

Upright and slightly
off the ground
the two of us
face off
now powerless

before the necessity of birds—
that they peck & prick
into a living reticle
our daily air.

MY SON REMEMBERS THE SUN

So often when I speak about the sun, an enormous red rose entangles itself in my tongue. But I do not have the capacity to remain silent. —Odysseus Elytis

So, in the redwood grove when we talked about dying
you said "I would really miss my mind" and
I knew exactly what you meant. I nodded "Yeah,
assembling your own mind through a lifetime
is like creating a new person from scratch."
You grinned, "Dying seems so wasteful after all that work."

You and I had talked about this. How a single day should be enough—
or less for the two yellow butterflies
chasing each other round and round a distant fir;
maybe one orbit = one year.

"Details ..." you continued, "it's all in the details, and God
is a big-picture guy. Up there—." You pointed, and stopped.
We were under a tree so tall the sun hung just above
the tip, slowly unfolding its tarp of hourly motes, spilling them
onto our knees. We had abandoned the hike to sit
on a slope so steep our chins were tilted 45 degrees.
There came into my head then, all at once, a way to explain
the essential difference between right-and-left, and east-and-west.
This is what I need to say to him—your brother, not you.
I took a breath to speak.

But you stood up, covered in almost-horizontal light
leaning your head back, facing the fractured sky. "If there were
a god, wouldn't it *have to be* the sun?" I turned slightly,
to face the nearest tree. I had just touched its airy outer bark
and knew I was miles from the central core. *Which might be fire. Or not.*
Which I must now spend another lifetime trying to reach.

"*That's* why we need so many minds!" I said softly,
"so we can go slowly enough, handing off in relays,"
but you stayed silent, nailed
by a single beam, before I could add
"You and I have talked about this," though we hadn't yet.

14

GEOGRAPHY LESSON

Between a map
as big as the earth
and the earth

must be a different kind of air.

Like the silences
inside a piece of music, or
the crawl space
out of the nucleus of every atom
to its rim.

        Within these particulate regions of air
anything, anything . . ..

STILL THE ANIMALS

Half buried in the murk
where the paint drizzles down
behind the frame—.

See the animals standing
along the bottom of the painting

                a solemn level row
of paws, claws, hooves, and shell,
their colors pale, their bodies
here bravely and hastily assembled.

                   The turtle
is speaking
with its feet. They plead
mute as empty teacup saucers

from the bottom of the painting where,
gazing out from under
the caved-in floor,
      the contoured highway
             shoulder, the collapsing city,

gently these animals
ride the rim of our oblivion,
gently they exceed its limits.

Unable

or unwilling
to founder with the other
more deeply-buried things, they are
every one, still showing,

their familiar proportions
chime wanly in the dusk
magnified beyond
whatever they might have previously

                   said.

AND IF THE DEAD DO DREAM

The I standing in the street
has slipped out the second-story window
from the I in the bed half asleep

a kind of peeling down of speech so it falls around the feet.

Having ascertained that the glass of poems
on the kitchen sill has not yet
been tampered with

between wimple of dusk, nun-shape of evening

we ride into the dreaming minds of the dead.
Our horse nods into a knelt wind.

Our rivulet hearts granted amnesty,
we have enough hard bread to last us
the whole way

playing out our rope

to draw across
the hull of each star-barn
we gallop past.

I for the slow remedy
I for the full sleep.

PRACTICE FABLE

If the animal is the first idea, the second must be the house
—my house

My house creaks at night.
Randomly. Loudly. Waking me up.

And why, unless the soil be mobile
and the house stiff?

And why, unless the ground is leaving and the house
trying to follow, staggers?

and why, unless the earth's a giant turning in her sleep?

My backside against the mattress—all night
tiny earthquakes
strum me.

I know no story for this.

And what ails you, my house—?

your limbs still wholly
unfurl-
able.

The giant moves beneath you, but will not waken until—what?
        She may greet guests at the door of her castle?
        You are that castle?
        There is no more wounded king?

The house practicing
        in its sleep.

AS TREE

listen with your feet

don't cough

climb onto a stump
and wait for
its phantom trunk
to pin you to the sky

look into, into, into
(not down-on or over-at)
until you feel your face
moving forward without you

kidnapped back
by its original family
but gently so

swoop, and
(oh, intransitively)
fling

WHERE DID YOU GROW UP?

When people say, "Where did you grow up?" I want to be accurate.
At the bottom of a road made from a rose-colored stone.
A group of small houses there, not terribly distinct.

When people say, "Where are you from?" I want to be honest.
A place where air remained transparent, and completely blue.
There were flowers near the houses, and the smaller rocks,
all shades of sunrise.

How can I say I grew up
in a place I've never been?

No stores nearby, a round church
on one of the slopes. Up there the grasses
were always falling over, which made us fall down too,
and sink into their gold and silver heaps that filled
our eyes so full of blades and didn't blind us. I can still remember
the kind of breaking noise they made
on all the days it never rained for months.

Here are some things: There were mostly no trees.
The colors were roses from the ground and from the air, pale blue.
This holds up. I can walk in these colors anywhere,
breathing them like chalk dust,
like reflected light from the sky-eating mountains.

A tree stood by a wall in someone's garden; it was an apricot.
There was a bench underneath, a small table nearby.
The leaves were yellow in autumn, and fell off on a single day in November.
I was never there in winter.

I remember the children playing together, but I don't know anyone else
who grew up there. And yes, the water,
welled into a little pool beside a rock.

CRITICAL MASS

Upon an early January afternoon
resolve to leave this house

you've stayed in far too long
beneath a ceiling-mosaic of broken glass.

This time you must at least approach the door
because when you glanced up just now, past

the familiar pleach of shards,
somebody with an apron on

was sweeping marbles from under bar stools
above your head; and now you hear

(seeping through the widening cracks)
two rival lovers singing the opening duet
from *The Pearl Fishers*.

The beauty coalesces; the beauty's much too apt.

Your ceiling keens and spins—a chanticleer.
Threatens to shatter into a heart.

DEAR BAOBAB,

Laughter keeps stopping me,
and I remain unable
to untangle myself
from the minnow-like shenanigans
of its mirrors.
I have seen many red things in my kitchen

but never with such girth,
such derangement of parts
working as a single vegetable—.
                    Surely your race began
as a frantic stashing
of all the earlier versions of the sun.

For sure I want to raise a glass, deep within
that bar your ancestor once hollowed
out of itself,
where elephant clientele, foolishly ecstatic,
discarded their trunks outside
in piles and piles.

Love, Anita

WHEN SUMMER SOLSTICE GOES ON A BIT TOO LONG

From an alcove in the corner of the barn
an invisible piano *plocks* and *plings* its bottle-cap notes
across the threshing floor.
The hens around their crushed corn
begin to teeter, pirouette.

The hay in the empty stalls
rises a few centimeters to eavesdrop, hears
only sorrow, sorrow, sorrow from the pocky
shadows, but its winter ears are thin and stale.

Replete with lavender and roses, bees
overrule with a descant from the loft.

Softly, prematurely, an ash tree behind the barn
is shedding its August blither
of crisp light yellow leaves
so it can follow the poor piano back

a century to a quiet afternoon in Greece
where the deluded instrument now
executes short snuffling chords to remind us
of the pigs under the nearby olive trees.

The local chicken pitch has gone up
at least an octave above the bees',
though the rooster seems oblivious as he
struts in and out the tiny door from the dark stall
to the newly dappled yard.

EARLY KNOWLEDGE

In paradise Adam stubbed his toe on a rock.
It bled and bled, until, at the snake's suggestion
he wrapped it in a poultice of dampened leaves
from the Forbidden Tree, thus gaining
through osmosis
a wholly different kind of knowledge.

After Adam's foot healed he
could walk across hot coals and not be burned.

Everywhere the family went outside the walls
the sun was local,
already had a name like Hank
or That-Which-Makes-Rocks-Steam.

The moon too, and most of
the animals had different names
than the ones he first gave them.

But with his new knowledge
Adam could go deeper.
Earth, Air, Fire, Water—he broke them down
into smaller and smaller parts:
      electron   proton   Higgs boson
neutrino   quark . . ..

In his final decades
Adam went over to naming horses
thus assuring an endless supply for future races.
Eve would find him
      evenings
under the village bougainvillea
reciting into his beer
      Black Caviar   Asteroid   Crucifix
      Awesome Feather   Bustin Stones   Queen's Logic
            Wounded Knee . . ..

Eve took a lover from one of the Nephilim.

MESSAGING

The white tee shirts are pegged up
shoulder to shoulder along the length
of the clothesline. Fresh. Gently swaying.

        And I am the one
                to decide

if they have something to say
for themselves in a way we are able
to hear.
      And since, at length

I can discern no essentials to convey

                  for them,
a vacancy remains.

            I give it away
      to a herd of African elephants
listening with their feet.

They stand
shoulder to shoulder

all undulating ears, all
looking off into the distance, each
resting extra weight on both front legs

    with one foot
barely raised, slightly tilted—
to catch those long, low vibrations
coming through the ground.

COMMON GROUND

I was planting carrot seeds on my balcony
and one thing led to another.

Each tiny seed fell by intention, landed
by whim.

The early spring forest flames again
with dragons in varying degrees

of wakefulness.
Out on the forest trail I pause to greet

an enormous Douglas Fir, grandfather
to many, whose bark I have come to know

as a test of visual memory,
each proportioned segment a new prime.

This time the tree steps forward
half a dimension or so, and I spill

into that framed unlidded vestibule
as if I were ash sown

at the brink of rampage
athwart the eye-slits of an ever-burgeoning heave
                              of sunsets.

I PETITION THE LEAF

Let us start with limes in their heaven.
Let us balance this with deeply-rooted stones

        upthrust—. In the up-here
we are asking
our moving green waters to keep you soft
not molten.

The whole house of us is a ship crossing the green;
        our riggings
plunder the moat at its margin.

I know your ancestors have sometimes brawled into rocks.

I know buried mountains in Arabia
that would eat our breath and dissolve
           into rivers of chalk.

Up here, our world a massive hierarchy
of dazzlings.

If we slipped a knife around all sunlight's edges,
lifted out
the surrounding darks
we too would know
        sunlight as a shaped thing,

a new planet poised, a house
overlapping.

But for you,

tiny red leaf—fan-lobed, veined,
        involute—fallen onto my knee
through the open window of my car,
when I pick you up by your plump-but-sinewy
        stem

the twirl reflex takes full control
of my body
funneling all thought into
        finger and thumb.

THE FIRST BRIDGE

One sun trumped by two drops of water.
On this remote forest path I see only
          through dripping trees, only by the mercy of the normal,
the steadily drowning light (not heavy) light.

As my feet hit the bridge and start a hollow clumping,
          below it
an unusually small squirrel starts to cross a log.
He looks up—oh exactly—as I look down.
We are like a duo of marionettes.
Then in that tethered way of squirrels, he swivels
          to pick his way
amid chunks of wood, leaves, moss, and
                    disappears
although something is caught in a net
that my heart seems to have been harboring.

I had closed my eyes to see if I would know without looking
when the squirrel disappeared, and I would not.

His proportions were perfect, his tiny feet, his tail
curled over his head to steady him, his brown and grey and slight
red against the yellows and greens, everything
squirrel size down there, the stones arranged for his rummagings.
In what way does he know how beautiful he is?
I only have a filament sense of this.
That his knowing is part of why it works.

BAOBAB: AN ELEGY

O for a world based on baobabs!

Underneath-branches would be our primary way of doing things.

Light would come to us riding every preposition, not just up to down,
    because so much light *originates* within the bark, the boles, the substance
    of these trees.

Not in an overt sense, like lamps. More vast.

These trees are innately upside down, and so seem comical. Maybe this is
    their way
of being truly serious. Their roots are on their heads, as hearts are on
    sleeves.

Just knowing they were abundantly hither and yon would so lighten our
    lives
that we would be accustomed to walking *beneath* our floating hearts.

We would feed cucumbers to the baobabs by raising our arms as high as we
    could
with a slice sticking out between thumb and index finger.

Such acts are essential, lest we become like collapsed stars.

Formerly barren hillsides would be pricked out with those "uncle" baobabs
    who are shaped
like people without waists.

The trees seem not to be natives of Earth, but have been here so long one
    wonders why they
never caught on. Wherever they came from seems a much better place.

Their roots splay above-ground openly and shamelessly around the trunks,
    like extra body parts from ill-defined species all basking contentedly in
    the sun.

Their trunks are made up of pocks, knobs, wrinkles, blobs, as if children
were once encouraged to pelt them with handfuls of rocks and mud,
which were cheerfully welcomed as ballast. The trees are contused.
Somehow this gives comfort to the rest of us, trying so hard to remain
smooth.

Baobabs are said to live in herds. Elephants strip and eat their bark, and in
the process
heedlessly metamorphose into trees, over and over. But baobabs are never
elephants
standing still.

Their vulnerability shows in how they eat light when it moves horizontally
through the land like flame in the grasses. Such an appetite is terrifying
for them, who already have light enough of their own.

ACKNOWLEDGMENTS

Thanks to the editors of the following journals and books in which these poems first appeared:

"Baobab: An Elegy," as "Baobabia." *Weekly Hubris* (www.weeklyhubris.com). Feb. 18, 2013.

"Early Knowledge." *The Dark Mountain Project: Book Five.* April 2014.

"The Land Renews Its Role as Horse." *Bear Deluxe #36.* Fall 2014.

"Leaf Dancing." *Weekly Hubris.* Oct. 1, 2015.

"Prayer of a Refugee." *Red Savina Review.* Fall, 2016.

NOTES

"A Taxonomy of Grieving"   5

I wrote this shortly after my husband died, when I saw on my brother's refrigerator a list of Shakespeare's plant taxonomy, and I realized suddenly that the witches in *Macbeth* were actually dancing around a cauldron of herbs, not the parts of animals! Somehow it was comforting to think that the odd magic of giving the same name to two things that bore some hidden resemblance, could be the key to me once again seeing the world as a beautiful place.

Shakespeare's taxonomy (a partial list)

Eye of Newt = Mustard Seed
Toe of Frog = Buttercup
Wool of Bat = Holly Leaves
Lizard Leg = Ivy
A Hawk's Heart = Wormwood
Bear's Foot = Lady's Mantle
Calf's Snout = Snapdragon
Sparrow's Tongue = Knotweed

"Practice Fable"   19

The first half of the epigraph is from Wallace Stevens.

"Wounded king" refers to the Fisher King in the Grail legend, whose unhealed wound was responsible for keeping the world in a state of perpetual drought. There is also, in this short list, the hint that giants have long been presented in stories as monsters, and maybe it's time to be done with that myth.

"Early Knowledge"   25

The idea for this came when I started reading Australian Aborigine tales, and found that practically every tribe had its own name for the sun and the moon, and it struck me as it so often has before that gods are really quite local, at least in the beginning: they have terroir, like wines!

BIOGRAPHY

Throughout her life Anita Sullivan has found ways to revel in music, poetry, and the natural world. These passions, combined with a barely-under-control humor, have formed the substance of her literary career. Her first book of essays, *The Seventh Dragon: The Riddle of Equal Temperament*, was an exploration and meditation on the tuning system used on modern pianos. It won the Western States Book Award for creative nonfiction in 1986. Since then, she has published a travel essay book, *Ikaria: A Love Odyssey on a Greek Island*, two poetry chapbooks, a full-length poetry collection *Garden of Beasts*, a novel *Ever After*, and many on and offline book reviews, essays, and poems. For 26 years she has been active in the literary community of Oregon's Willamette Valley.

www.ingramcontent.com/pod-product-compliance
Lightning Source LLC
Chambersburg PA
CBHW022348040426
42449CB00006B/780